All Good Things Come To An End: How To Close A Negotiation

How To Develop The Skill Of Closing In Order To Get The Best Possible Outcome From A Negotiation

"Practical, proven techniques that will help you get the best deal possible out of your next negotiation"

Dr. Jim Anderson

Published by:

Blue Elephant Consulting

Tampa, Florida

Printed in the United States of America

Library of Congress Control Number: 2015917391

ISBN-13: 978-1518661693

ISBN-10: 1518661696

Warning – Disclaimer

The purpose of this book is to educate and entertain. This book does not promise or guarantee that anyone following the ideas, tips, suggestions, techniques or strategies will be successful. The author, publisher and distributor(s) shall have neither liability nor responsibility to anyone with respect to any loss or damage caused, or alleged to be caused, directly or indirectly by the information contained in this book.

Recent Books By The Author

Product Management

- Product Management Secrets: Techniques For Product Managers To Boost Product Sales And Increase Customer Satisfaction

- Customer Lessons For Product Managers: Techniques For Product Managers To Better Understand What Their Customers Really Want

Public Speaking

- Secrets To Organizing A Speech For Maximum Impact: How to put together a speech that will capture and hold your audience's attention

- How To Become A Better Speaker By Changing How You Speak: Change techniques that will transform a speech into a memorable event

CIO Skills

- What CIOs Need To Know About Working With Partners: Techniques For CIOs To Use In Order To Be Able To Successfully Work With Partners

- How CIOs Can Make Innovation Happen: Tips And Techniques For CIOs To Use In Order To Make Innovation Happen In Their IT Department

IT Manager Skills

- Secrets Of Managing Budgets: What IT Managers Need To Know In Order To Understand How Their Company Uses Money

- Growing Your CIO Career: How CIOs Can Work With The Entire Company In Order To Be Successful

Negotiating

- Learn How To Package Trades In Your Next Negotiation

- Learn How To Signal In Your Next Negotiation: How To Develop The Skill Of Effective Signaling In A Negotiation In Order To Get The Best Possible Outcome

Miscellaneous

- The Internet-Enabled Successful School District Superintendent: How To Use The Internet To Boost Parental Involvement In Your Schools

- Power Distribution Unit (PDU) Secrets: What Everyone Who Works In A Data Center Needs To Know!

Note: See a complete list of books by Dr. Jim Anderson at the back of this book.

.

Acknowledgements

Any book like this one is the result of years of real-world work experience. In my over 25 years of working for 7 different firms, I have met countless fantastic people and I've been mentored by some truly exceptional ones. Although I've probably forgotten some of the people who made me the person that I am today, here is my attempt to finally give them the recognition that they so truly deserve:

- Thomas P. Anderson
- Art Puett
- Bobbi Marshall
- Bob Boggs

Dr. Jim Anderson

This book is dedicated to my family: Lori, Maddie, Nick, and Ben. None of this would have been possible without their constant love and support.

Thanks for always believing in me and providing me with the strength to always be willing to go out there and be my best for you.

Table Of Contents

Great Deals Are A Result Of The Trades That We Package

The part of a negotiation that every negotiator wants to get to as quickly as possible is the closing. This is when your prize is insight: the deal that you want is so close that you could almost reach out and touch it. However, it turns out that this is the most dangerous part of a negotiation – it can all slip away from you if you don't know how to navigate the closing correctly.

Negotiating is a skill that we hone by using it over and over again. Opportunities to practice our negotiating skills come in all shapes and sizes and buying a car is one such event. Another way to get better at this thing that we call negotiating is by watching what other profession negotiators do. Negotiations between businesses and their workers, such as Verizon and the CWA / IBEW or even between two businesses such as EA and Take Two can offer us important learning experiences.

In labor negotiations, it's the balance of power that can often determine which side walks away from the bargaining table with the best deal. Over at Boeing with the large number of different unions that the company has to deal with this has been shown to be true over and over again.

In order to be able to successfully close a negotiation, you need to have built up a strong foundation that will allow you to move the negotiation to a close. This involves building rapport with the other side of the table and also knowing just exactly who is calling the shots for the other side.

Finally, the closing of a negotiation often comes about because of a deadline or perhaps because both parties have reached a deadlock that they can't resolve. In both cases, your ability to get the deal that you want will be at risk. Knowing how to deal with these situations is a core skill that every negotiator needs to master.

For more information on what it takes to be a great negotiator, check out my blog, The Accidental Negotiator, at:

www.TheAccidentalNegotiator.com

Good luck!

- Dr. Jim Anderson

About The Author

I must confess that I never set out to be a negotiator. When I went to school, I studied Computer Science and thought that I'd get a nice job programming and that would be that. Well, at least part of that plan worked out!

My first job was working for Boeing on their F/A-18 fighter jet program. I spent my days programming fighter jet software in assembly language and I loved it. The U.S. government decided to save some money and went looking for other countries to sell this plane to. This put me into an unfamiliar role: I started to negotiate with foreign military officials and I ended up having to participate in the negotiations for large international deals.

Time moved on and so did I. I found myself working for Siemens, the big German telecommunications company. They were making phone switches and selling them to the seven U.S. phone companies. The problem was that the switches were too complicated. When it came time to negotiate a deal with the customer, the sales teams struggled to create an effective negotiating strategy. I was called in to bridge the world between the product functionality and the business impacts as they related to the negotiations.

I've spent over 25 years working as a negotiator for both big companies and startups. This has given me an opportunity to learn what it takes to both plan and execute negotiations of all sizes. When it comes to negotiations, I've pretty much been there, done that.

I now live in Tampa Florida where I spend my time managing my consulting business, Blue Elephant Consulting, teaching college courses at the University of South Florida, and traveling to work with companies like yours to share the knowledge that I have about how to prepare for and execute successful negotiations.

I'm always available to answer questions and I can be reached at:

Dr. Jim Anderson
Blue Elephant Consulting
Email: jim@BlueElephantConsulting.com
Facebook: http://goo.gl/1TVoK
Web: **www.BlueElephantConsulting.com**

"Unforgettable communication skills that will set your ideas free..."

Create An Effective Negotiating Team At Your Company!

Dr. Jim Anderson is available to provide training and coaching on the topics that are the most important to people who have to negotiate: how can my team effectively prepare for and execute a successful negotiation that will get us what we both want and need?

Dr. Anderson believes that in order to both learn and remember what he says, audiences need to laugh. Each one of his speeches is full of fun and humor so that what he says "sticks" with everyone.

Dr. Anderson's Negotiating Training Includes:

1. How to plan for a negotiation: what information do you need and where can you find it?

2. What's the best way to explore how a deal can be created during a negotiation?

3. How can you bring a negotiation to a close without giving in to the other side?

Dr. Jim Anderson works with over 100 customers per year. To invite Dr. Anderson to work with you, contact him at:

Phone: 813-418-6970 or
Email: jim@BlueElephantConsulting.com

11

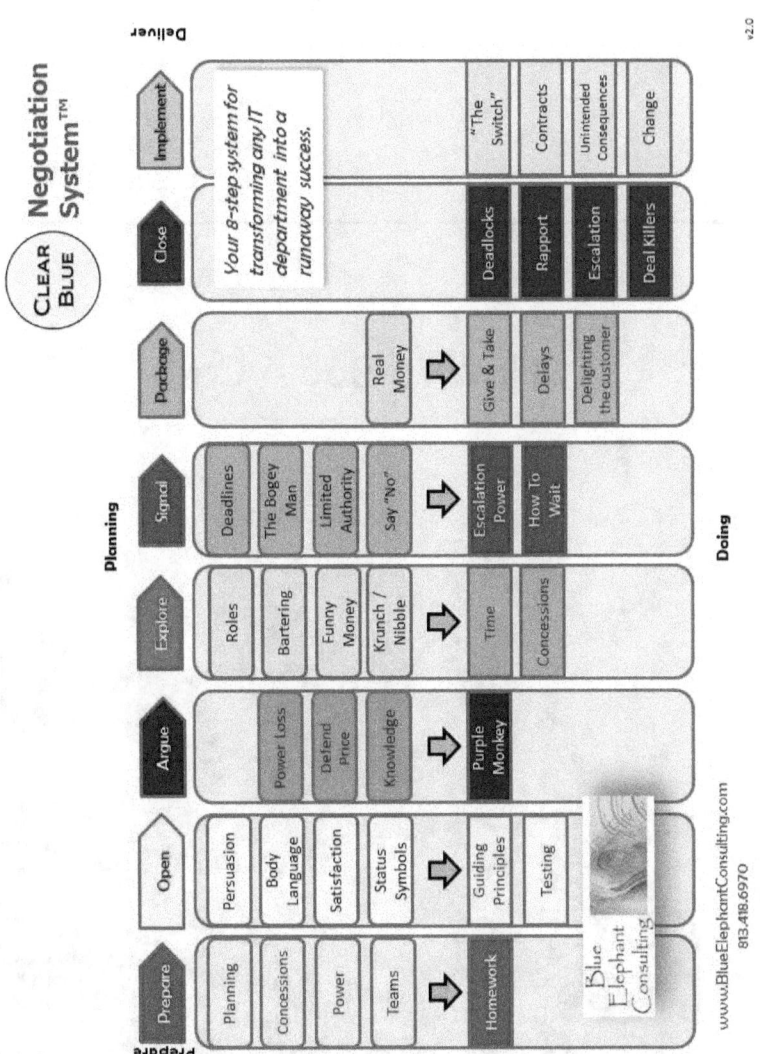

CLEAR BLUE Negotiation System™

v2.0

Your 8-step system for transforming any IT department into a runaway success.

Prepare	Open	Argue	Explore	Signal	Package	Close	Implement
Planning	Persuasion	Power Loss	Roles	Deadlines			
Concessions	Body Language	Defend Price	Bartering	The Bogey Man			
Power	Satisfaction	Knowledge	Funny Money	Limited Authority	Real Money		
Teams	Status Symbols		Krunch / Nibble	Say "No"			
Homework	Guiding Principles	Purple Monkey	Time	Escalation Power	Give & Take	Deadlocks	"The Switch"
	Testing		Concessions	How To Wait	Delays	Rapport	Contracts
					Delighting the customer	Escalation	Unintended Consequences
						Deal Killers	Change

Prepare → Planning → Doing → Deliver

Blue Elephant Consulting

www.BlueElephantConsulting.com
813.418.6970

The **Clear Blue Negotiation System™** has been created to provide negotiators with a clear roadmap for how to manage a successful negotiation. This system shows negotiators what needs to be done and in what order to do it.

13

Chapter 1

How To Buy A Car

Chapter 1: How To Buy A Car

So let's spend some time talking about something that every negotiator can relate to: buying a car. It's all good and fine to talk about negotiating concepts, but buying a car is when the (pardon the pun) rubber really hits the road.

Nobody that I know ever looks forward to the whole process of buying a car. Although they want a car, they don't want the hassle that they have to go through to get one. For the purposes of this discussion, we won't care if you are looking for a new or a used car — the process is basically the same. Let's see if we can make things just a bit easier for you the next time you need to go car shopping:

1. **Determine Your Schedule**: This will set the tone for the whole car buying process: how much time do you have before you need to have a car? The more time that you have before you need to make a decision, the more power you have. If you currently have a car to drive or if you walk/bike/run everywhere and can keep doing so, then you are (another pun) in the driver's seat.

   You can take your time in selecting the brand, model, and sales location that you want to buy from. If things aren't going your way at any time, you can just stop the process and restart it whenever it suits you. On the other hand, if your clunker just gave up the ghost and you really need a new set of wheels, like yesterday, then you have less negotiating power, but you can maximize what power you do have.

   You do this by spending more time on the car search right now and doing your research thoroughly and moving quickly. If you spend more time now, then you'll have all of the information that you need and you can lead the negotiations.

2. **Find Out What You Want**: As you know, negotiations can't start until you decide exactly what you want. If you already know, then great, move on to the next step. If you don't know, then this is the time to do some off-line research and then go do some test driving. No matter what the "helpful" salesperson says, keep in mind that you are not a car buyer right now — you are a car researcher and so your one and only job is to decide what make and model you want. Don't sweat options and maintenance packages right now — just pick a car!

3. **Research How Much This Car Should Cost**: Ah, isn't living in the 21st Century grand? Thanks to the power of the Internet you can go online and quickly find out how much your dealer paid for the car. A great place to start is Edmunds.com. If you need to understand the difference between Manufacturer's Suggested Retail Price, Dealer Invoice price, etc., then checkout an excellent overview at WikiAnswers. Once you know what a reasonable price is, then you are ready to negotiate.

4. **Own The Stage**: When you go to a car dealer to start negotiating, it is as though you are walking onto a stage. This is one of the reasons that so many people fear buying a car — they've got stage fright.

   Ideally you want the salesperson to be eager to talk to you so you should do you best to set things up in your favor. We all know that car dealers want to move as much inventory as possible before the end of the month/year. If you can wait until that time is drawing close, then you'll improve your position. No matter what, make sure that you have all the time in the world to talk to the car dealer because that will put you in control of the discussion. The salesperson won't have the same amount of time and so you'll be in control.

5. **<u>The Last Word Said Is The Most Important</u>**: Realize that even after you've reached a fair price for your car, the salesperson is still participating in the negotiating game — it's not over yet. You need to stay awake and engaged because this is where the money can slip out of your wallet / purse. Taxes, documentation, dealer prep are all negotiable items and the salesperson is going to want to present them to you as fixed items. Don't give up now!

Chapter 2

Real Life Negotiating Lessons: Verizon vs. The CWA & IBEW

Chapter 2: Real Life Negotiating Lessons: Verizon vs. The CWA & IBEW

In case you haven't been watching the news lately, the telecommunications giant Verizon has been locked in labor negotiations with the Communication Workers of America (CWA) and the International Brotherhood of Electrical Workers (IBEW). Both sides of this negotiation are run by professional negotiators who have done this countless times before. What this means for us is that it offers a great chance to learn from the masters.

What I'd like to draw your attention to today is the use of deadlines as a negotiating technique. We've talked about deadlines here before; however, it's always even more instructive to see it at work in the real world.

The two sides had been going at it for several weeks when the CWA and IBEW announced that if an agreement was not reached by Monday, ...strike action then becomes possible....

Verizon's Chief Communications Officer, Peter Thonis, then was quoted as saying that the company was ...very surprised, given the situation. So what was going on here?

An interesting clue can be found in a comment that the CWA/IBEW made to the press in which they stated that progress had been "slow". What we are seeing here is a classic negotiating end game move – the unions are signaling to Verizon that they want to wrap up negotiations. By all accounts, progress on the key issues had been made and things were drawing to a close anyway. By issuing this ultimatum, the unions were sure to get the attention of Verizon's senior management.

It's a good guess that the senior management on both sides were probably not involved in the long hours of nitty gritty negotiations that were taking place between the two sides. This this the type of task that is best left to lawyers and other professional negotiators. However, by sending this signal, the unions clearly communicated that it was time for senior management on both sides to return to the table.

Without actually being at the table it's hard to say exactly where things stood. However, a good guess would be that the nitty gritty workers had gotten as far as they could. What could be resolved had been and what was still unresolved could not be resolved at their level. By calling the senior management back to the table, the hope was that the last few items could be resolved and the negotiations could be wrapped up.

What should you take away from all of this? Simply that a deadline has another role in negotiations — as a communications tool. Note that neither side appeared to be very angry with the other side, instead they were using the deadline as a way to mark the end of one phase of the negotiations and the start of the end game.

Chapter 3

Do You Want To Play A Game? EA & Take-Two's Negotiating Failure

Chapter 3: Do You Want To Play A Game? EA & Take-Two's Negotiating Failure

At this blog, we firmly believe that the best negotiating learning comes from observing the real world – not from just reading yet-another-book-on-negotiating. Thankfully, there continue to be a number of fantastic stories in the news that provide key lessons on how companies negotiate with each other and, all too often, what goes wrong...

Set the scene. The players in this particular ongoing drama were Electronic Arts (EA) and Take-Two Interactive Software. EA is a well-known developer of video games for a number of different platforms. EA has a number of very popular titles including the best-selling "Madden Football". Take-Two is a young upstart firm that sells the insanely popular "Grand Theft Auto" games. Our story really starts seven months ago when EA made an unsolicited bid of $2B for Take-Two.

So what happened? Take-Two basically said "Thanks, but no thanks." They stated that they thought that the EA offer of $25.74/share was too low. One reason that they said this was because their most recent game, Grand Theft Auto iV, had already sold over 10M copies.

What happened next? EA ended up letting its hostile takeover bid expire. However, as recently as this August it still seemed as though a deal might be had. EA announced that they were entering into confidential discussions with Take-Two during which EA would have access to non-public info about Take-Two's business plans.

Where do things stand now? EA has announced that they will not make another offer for Take-Two.

What happened here? Underneath all of the discussions of how to merge two large software firms was a ticking time-bomb: the Christmas season. From the beginning, EA had made it clear that in order for the deal to make sense for them, they would have had to have been able to integrate the Take-Two product catalog into the EA catalog in time for the Christmas season. What this meant is that a deal would have had to been inked by mid-September in order to allow enough time for this to happen.

What can we learn from this failed deal? If there is a schedule issue, then you need to stay aware of it during the entire negotiation. The other side of this coin is that if you don't want a deal to happen (like Take-Two) then simply by dragging your feet you can cause the deal to go away.

Chapter 4

Wachovia, Wells Fargo, and Citigroup – Now You're Negotiating With The Big Boys

Chapter 4: Wachovia, Wells Fargo, and Citigroup – Now You're Negotiating With The Big Boys

The financial world sure seems to be intent on driving itself off of a cliff; however, that is no reason that negotiations should stop. As long as companies are talking, there is learning for us to be doing. This time around the negotiations center on just who gets to buy what remains of the battered Wachovia bank – Wells Fargo or Citigroup? Sounds like it's time for some negotiating...

I guess just a little bit of background would be appropriate so that we're all on the same page here. Wachovia is a bank that made the mistake of investing too heavily in securities that were backed by sub-prime mortgages. Once folks started defaulting on those mortgages, Wachovia's investments went up in smoke and they could no longer get credit to cover their debts. They had to put themselves up for sale or risk going out of business. Interestingly enough, the FDIC stepped in and brokered a deal with Citigroup to buy out Wachovia. This allowed Wachovia to keep their doors open. Simple, eh?

Nothing ever stays simple in the world of finance for long. Wells Fargo realized that this was a great way to expand their operations on the cheap and so then they stepped in and offered more money than Citigroup to buy Wachovia. Oh oh – conflict.

Once both offers were on the table, the negotiating started. Needless to say it didn't go well. In fact, things were going so poorly, that all three sides ended up calling for a two-day timeout. The purpose of this timeout was to give everyone a chance to step back from the negotiation table and take a breather. Another big reason that the timeout was called was because the government was not happy at how the negotiations were going – they were taking too long.

Now just between us, what do you think that the negotiators did during those two days? Sit at home? Huddled with just their team to plot strategy? No way! I'm sure that all three teams reached out behind each other's backs and had private discussions with the other two teams. This "forced pause" in the negotiations was just a bit unusual, but the experienced negotiator knows to make the best of what he/she has been handed. This two day period was just what the teams needed in order to send up some trial balloons and see what the other side thought of them. They could also do some probing in order to determine if there was any sort of offer that they could make that would effectively make the other side walk away.

In the end, this last step is exactly what happened. Just before the two-day timeout was called, there had been a deal on the table that would have split up Wachovia with Citigroup taking Wachovia's northeast customers and assets and Wells Fargo taking the rest. However, because of the way that the deal had been structured and because they had two days to think about it, Citigroup eventually decided that they would be taking on too much risk for too little of a benefit if they agreed to this deal. In the end, Citigroup walked away and Wells Fargo will now buy out all of Wachovia.

From a negotiating point-of-view, the two-day timeout made all of the difference. Before the break, Citigroup was willing to go toe-to-toe with Wells Fargo. However, the two day break gave them time to change their mind and in the end, that made all the difference in the world.

Chapter 5

Boeing Strike Is Over: Did Negotiation Save The Day

Chapter 5: Boeing Strike Is Over: Did Negotiation Save The Day?

Just in case you had not heard, the Association of Machinists and Aerospace Workers has settled its strike with Boeing. The machinists had been off the job and on the picket lines for 52 days – a very long time for a Boeing strike. Both sides are calling the agreement that they came to as being a "fair compromise". But was it? Let's take a closer look at how things worked out from a negotiating point-of-view and see what we think happened...

One of the key components of the negotiated agreement is that this contract will cover 4 years unlike previous contracts which have covered only 3 years. This was very important to Boeing because in three years they will just be reaching the peak of production for their new 787 jet and the possibility of having another crippling strike occur then could damage the company's bottom line as well as their reputation.

The machinists union is actually fairly small – only 27,000 workers. However, they were negotiating from a position of strength. Boeing currently has 3,725 orders for new airplanes that need to be filled. It was rumored that the strike was costing Boeing $100M a day. The machinists were also helped by the fact that the type of work that they perform is highly specialized and not easily replaced. The work done by the machinists has a direct bearing on the final safety of the finished product and this is something that Boeing needs to make sure never gets compromised.

Boeing had bigger issues to consider during their negotiations with the machinists. Boeing is getting ready to face another contract renegotiation with the 21,000 strong Society of Professional Engineering Employees in Aerospace (SPEEA). This contract expires on December 1st so Boeing really needed to get the machinist strike wrapped up before they potentially had another strike on their hands. This also meant that Boeing could not just cave in to the machinists because then the SPEEA would be expecting the same.

Boeing has some other issues that had to be weighing on their decision making team. They were already going to have problems meeting their goal of delivering the first 787 Dreamliner planes in 2009. The lead time for getting a new plane design approved to be sold is quite lengthy. After Boeing has been able to assemble several of the first 787 planes, they will then need to start almost a year of around-the-clock flight testing.

So who walked away with what in the final contract?

It sure looks like the machinists got what they wanted. Specifically, Boeing agreed to limit its use of contractors doing work that machinists had previously done. Contractors will still be able to deliver parts to the production lines; however, the machinists will be in charge of tracking and distributing those parts once they enter the factory. I believe that this was the key point of the negotiations – if Boeing had been able to expand the role of contractors, then they would have been able to use fewer machinists. However, it looks like in order to end the strike quickly, Boeing backed away from this demand.

What's a negotiator to learn from all of this? Your negotiating power is not always obvious. The machinists were in a powerful situation and they knew it. They used this as leverage to prevent Boeing from reducing their importance and ensured that the next time they enter into a negotiation, they will be well positioned to get what they want.

Chapter 6

---

6 Ways To Break A Negotiation Deadlock (Plus One More)

Chapter 6: 6 Ways To Break A Negotiation Deadlock (Plus One More)

So how many times has this happened to you: there you are happily negotiating along and then all of a sudden *bang* you run into an immovable deadlock. Some issue or some condition that neither you nor the other side of the table seem to be able to see eye-to-eye on just brings everything to a screeching halt.

Hmm, what's a negotiator to do? All too often negotiators bump heads for a while trying to convince the other side to change their minds and then give up when this turns out to not be possible. There has got to be a better way of handling this! It turns out that there is...

Here are six (plus one) techniques that the folks over at the Karrass institute recommend for dealing with the deadlocks that occur in negotiations:

1. **Change The Setting**: The negotiations up to this point have taking place at a specific location. If you now change the setting, then all of a sudden both sides will feel like they are starting a new round of negotiations. This means that all of the old assumptions about what would or would not work are (almost) thrown out the window. This fresh perspective might be just what both sides need to go back and revisit the issue that is causing the deadlock.

2. **Change The Negotiator(s)**: We are all so vain that we almost never consider this possibility, but it can be a powerful option. Sometimes we run into a deadlock because one or more of the negotiators who is involved in the discussions just can't find a different way to look at the situation. This is often the case if the negotiations have gone on for a long time. If you switch out the

negotiator, then you may find that the negotiations have taken a step back as the new negotiator works to establish a relationship with the other side of the table, but this might be just what is needed to move the discussions forward.

3. **Change Levels In The Organization**: Often times a deadlock is a result of the negotiating parties not having the authority needed to be able to suggest an alternative. If this is the case, then a good way to deal with the problem is to kick it up to higher powers. They may be able to quickly find areas in which they can bend and that could get the whole discussion back on track quickly.

4. **Provide Additional Information**: Each side of the table must have a reason for not being willing to budge on the deadlock issue. This reason is based on the information that they currently have. Sometimes bringing the information that you have based your position on and laying it out on the table before both parties can result in a change. The other side might point out that one of your assumptions is incorrect or they may be surprised to learn a fact that they didn't know about. Either way, this might be just what is needed to get things moving again.

5. **Go "Off The Record"**: Depending on the level of rapport that you have been able to build with the other side, this could be just what is needed. When you go off the record, you indicate to the other side that you are going to have a discussion with them about negotiating strategy that once completed will not be mentioned again. This is designed to show how much you trust the other side and to see if perhaps both sides of the table are trying to reach the same end point and are just getting tripped up by a minor issue. Careful with this

one, you might be tipping your hand too much or too early in the negotiations.

6. **Say "Let's Shift Into The Both Win Mode"**: Although this doesn't really mean anything by itself, it's a great way to communicate to the other side that you would like to find a way to create a solution that works for both sides. Just by indicating that this is what you are working towards can often be the spark that causes the other side to start to consider more possible ways around your deadlock….and I promised you one more way to break a negotiation deadlock and so here it is:

7. **Take A Break**: it sounds so simple that often we overlook it, but taking a break and stepping away from the table can often be the most powerful way to break a negotiation deadlock. We all have a tendency to get caught up in a negotiation when we are in the thick of it and our ability to think of creative ways to resolve deadlocks can decrease the longer that we've been negotiating. Taking a break might be just what the doctor ordered to get our creative juices flowing again.

Chapter 7

Boeing Uses Negotiation To Dodge Yet Another Strike

Chapter 7: Boeing Uses Negotiation To Dodge Yet Another Strike

Boeing's commercial aircraft division just wrapped up the longest strike that Boeing has had in over a decade. Its Machinists have agreed to go back to work after 57 days off of the job. The press was saying that the strike was costing Boeing over $100M a day because of delays in the 3,000+ orders that they have for new aircraft from their customers. Coming on the heels of that was the ugly fact that Boeing's contract with the 21,000 strong Society of Professional Engineering Employees in Aerospace was running out as of December 1st. Needless to say, it was time for Boeing to start to do some fast negotiating...

Already pre-negotiating posturing had started. On Thursday the engineering union had stated that it wanted its members to vote to authorize a strike. The purpose of this was to raise the pressure on Boeing's management. Things had started to get hotter as the engineers accused Boeing of stalling the talks. In all honesty, this is probably correct because Boeing was focused on trying resolve the machinists strike and probably had dedicated only minimal resources to starting talks with the engineers. However, things had gotten so rocky that a federal mediator had already been brought in. It's not known if this mediator was the same one that was helping out with the discussions between Boeing and the machinists.

In negotiations, timing is everything. The engineering union had started their negotiations with Boeing last month AFTER the machinist's strike had already halted production at Boeing. There were differences between what the two unions were negotiating with Boeing for. The machinists were most concerned about having their jobs replaced with contract workers. The engineers on the other hand realized that they had more specialized talents that could not easily be replaced.

This meant that their major concerns revolved around pay and benefits.

Boeing was most interested in negotiating to create a four year contract instead of the traditional three year contract. The reason for this is because in three years they are going to be at the peak of their production schedule for their new 787 Dreamliner airplane and they didn't want to have to worry about a strike crippling their ability to deliver planes to their customers – that would damage their reputation and hurt their bottom line.

I'm quite surprised that considering that the union was preparing to take a strike vote on Thursday that they were somehow able to resolve their differences with Boeing so quickly that they were recommending to their members over the weekend to accept the tentative deal that had been reached (apparently on Friday). What the heck happened? Details are not currently available; however, the union's negotiators were getting ready to present the deal to union management on Friday evening.

Since the union had such a strong hand and since Boeing was still reeling from the machinist's strike, I can only guess that Boeing basically gave in to the engineering union's demands. If that is true, then there is a big question as to if the union was truly asking for enough?

This is a unique time in history for Boeing – they've got more orders for planes than they know what to do with. From a negotiating point-of-view the unions are in a much stronger position during this round of negotiations than they will be in four years when there is not such a large backlog of orders. As a confirmation of this, Randy Tisseth who is Boeing's VP of commercial marketing has announced that the company "will probably feel downward pressure in terms of orders next year...". Only time will tell if everyone got what they were looking for out of this negotiation.

Chapter 8

Every Negotiation Needs A Rap(port) Star!

Chapter 8: Every Negotiation Needs A Rap(port) Star!

So here's something that will blow your mind: studies have shown that car shopping customers are willing to pay between $200 and $300 MORE for a car if during the negotiation process they became convinced that the salesperson was committed to their satisfaction.

Wow – talk about a successful negotiation for the salesperson. But wait, isn't the customer getting something out of this also – satisfaction. Think back over all of those deals in which you have been the customer and in which you walked away afterwards feeling less than satisfied. Perhaps nobody is getting taken for a ride here (sorry for the pun).

It's possible that the customer side in this type of deal can actually put a value on being made to feel satisfied: $200-$300. Hmm, if it's true when people are buying cars, just imagine what feeling satisfied must be worth when you are working on a much larger deal!

All this comes down to one thing: part of the price that is being negotiated is friendship and goodwill. Angry, bitter, combative negotiators will get beaten down on price each and every time. In all business negotiations we must remember that we are negotiating not only things (goods and services), but also attitudes.

As the car buying study shows, part of the price of any deal that you negotiate will include:

1. **Trust:** does the other side trust that you have been straight with them and that you will keep your word after the deal is signed?

2. **Friendship:** yes, friendship does still exist in the 21st Century. Does the other side believe that they have developed a relationship with you that will continue to exist after the negotiations are completed?

3. **Integrity:** would you do something that you knew was wrong? Would you sell a product or a service that you knew was flawed or wasn't going to meet a customer's needs?

4. **Goodwill:** do you have that intangible asset that makes the other side believe that you will do them no harm?

5. **Credibility:** does your track record support what you are saying?

6. **Authority:** do you really have the ability to deliver all that you have promised?

7. **Status:** are you the peer or the better of the other side – are you the right one for them to be negotiating with?

It's important to note that there is a HUGE difference between establishing rapport (a connection) with the other side vs. just being cooperative. Experiments have shown that when the other side is exploitative, they can easily take advantage of cooperative negotiators.

So where does all of this lead to? It's as simple as realizing that compatible attitudes between both sides of the negotiating table are needed in order to be able to reach solid, long-lasting agreements. In the end, there is no way that either side can trust what the other side has promised if the two sides can't trust each other.

Although they may not be listed on the list of bargaining points that you drew up before the negotiations started, everything that we've discussed including recognition, friendship, and trust are always items that are up for negotiation. It's well worth the extra time that it takes to make sure both sides walk way mutually satisfied.

Chapter 9

Succeed By Bringing The Ghost Whisperer To The Negotiation

Chapter 9: Succeed By Bringing The Ghost Whisperer To The Negotiation

So there you are, sitting across the table from the other side starting a negotiation. If only you are able to use your considerable negotiating talents to convince them that what you want is best for them, then you're sure to get what you want – right? Nope, it turns out that although you might think that it's just you and the other side talking, it turns out that room is actually crowded with negotiating ghosts that you're going to have to learn to talk to...

The other side of the table rarely represents just themselves. No matter if you are trying to buy a car from them or sell them a house, you are really talking with someone who is really part of a larger organization. This can be a whole company, a spouse, kids, a banker, etc.

What this means to you as a negotiator is that the other side is going to have to satisfy the demands of their extended team (upper management, sales, the union, the spouse, etc.). They are going to have make sure that everyone on their side has their needs met before they can reach an agreement with you.

Although there can be quite a mix of people whispering into the other side's ear, there are four common characteristics that all of these impacted parties will share:

1. **Not All Will Agree:** This means that there will be conflict among members of the same team. If they can't agree, then this will impact the other side's ability to agree to your proposals.

2. **Nobody Is The Same:** All of the different individuals that the other side is representing have different needs and different priorities. This may be why the other side

seems to be changing their direction so often.

3. **Not All Are Equal:** Although there may be multiple parties whispering into the other side's ear, not all of them have an equal role to play when it comes to making a final decision.

4. **Not All Benefit The Same:** Just as all are not equal, so too not all will benefit the same amount from whatever deal you are negotiating.

All of these Ghost Whisperer issues lead you, my dear negotiator, to one simple conclusion: you need to come up with a way to deal with all of these "negotiation ghosts". Here are four tips for doing so:

1. You need to find out who is really making the decision on each issue in the negotiation. Keep in mind that it might be a different person for each issue.

2. Make sure that you get commitments from the people behind the other side when it comes to the value of the thing that you are offering and the validity of your offer.

3. Have the fundamental realization that the other side will be unable to give you the "yes" that you are looking for until his people allow him to give it. This means that your job is really to help him to get them to give him permission.

4. Oh yeah, you've got the same issues – you are really negotiating on the behalf of many different parties. You need to be a good enough negotiator that you are able to get your people to approve your ability to reach an agreement with the other side.

Chapter 10

Deadline? We Don't Need No Stinkin Deadline...

Chapter 10: Deadline? We Don't Need No Stinkin Deadline...

What would the world of negotiating be without deadlines? I can tell you that Hollywood movies would lose a lot of their plot if the bad guys couldn't set impossible deadlines for our heroes to try to meet. What about real life – why do people use deadlines while negotiating?

It's actually pretty simple, a deadline is an effective communication tool. Deadlines can be used by either side to apply pressure to the other side and force them to make a choice. If the party that's under pressure chooses to accept the deadline, then the deal will be done. Otherwise, who knows?

You see, the trick with deadlines is that when you are presented with one you can never be quite sure that it's real. In the game of poker this is called bluffing. The one thing that we do know about a deadline is that if we accept it, everything will be resolved. However, there will always be that unanswered question as to what would have happened if we had not met the deadline...

One solid piece of advice is given by experienced negotiators: always be skeptical of any deadline that you encounter during a negotiation. These types of fixed time limits have a tendency to come and go.

Now having said this, you also have to realize that in real life sometimes a deadline is real. If you choose to not meet it, then you are running the very real risk that this may kill the deal once and for all.

In order to help you see your way through the deadline maze, here are three questions that you need to ask yourself anytime that you encounter a deadline during a negotiation:

1. **For The Other Side**: what deadlines do you know about that the other side has to live with? Do you know what will happen if they miss their deadlines?

2. **For You**: what deadlines have been placed on me by either my team, my organization, or myself? Will these deadlines limit how effective I can be during this negotiation?

3. **Renegotiation**: Is it possible for my team to renegotiate any of the deadlines that have been placed on us by our own people? Who says that we can or cannot?

As much as we all dread having the other side throw a deadline at us, we need to remember that deadlines are an effective tool that we have in our own bag of tricks. Studies of negotiations have been done and they have revealed that deadlines do one thing very well – they force the other side to make a decision.

All too often in a negotiation, things can be dragging on for too long. If you find yourself in this situation where the other side appears to be resisting making up their minds, then perhaps a deadline is called for.

This type of situation often shows up when the other side is faced with an especially difficult decision. They will drag their feet longer in order to avoid having to make up their mind. If you can convey to them that there is a sense of legitimacy to your deadline, then you can use this powerful tool to close the deal faster.

Chapter 11

A Sales Negotiator's Guide To Dealing With A Deadlock

Chapter 11: A Sales Negotiator's Guide To Dealing With A Deadlock

When driving a car, the #1 thing that most of us fear is hitting a wall. Or another car. Or pretty much anything that would cause us to come to a complete stop quickly. Why are we so afraid of this? Well duh – it will damage / destroy the car that we're in, delay or prevent us from getting to where we want to go, and may even result in damage to us. The same thing can happen during a negotiation, but we call it a deadlock.

A deadlock occurs when both sides have not yet reached an agreement and all of a sudden they reach an issue that they fundamentally cannot agree on. If negotiating was a board game, then there would be no possible moves for either side to take – deadlock.

If you are a negative person you might be willing to give up and walk away. Lots of people do. A deadlock is a powerful thing and it can affect both sides of the negotiating table in the following ways:

- A deadlock tests the resolve and the strength of both sides.

- A deadlock often forces both sides to be willing to give more concessions after it occurs.

- A deadlock is a signal to both sides of the table that what they want out of the negotiation might not be possible.

- A deadlock can cause both sides to reduce what they expect to get out of the negotiations.

- A deadlock can mess up schedules for both sides.

- A deadlock can make a negotiation more expensive and riskier for both sides.

So this all seems like it's pretty serious stuff. However, there's more.

Both sides of a negotiation realize going in that a deadlock can occur. The key thing that you as a negotiator need to determine is which side fears a deadlock more. Generally speaking, the larger an organization is and the more layers that it has in its management structure, the less able it is to deal with a deadlock. If you are willing to risk not walking away with a deal, then your negotiating power may be greater than the other side's.

No matter how much power you think that you have, what every negotiator needs to realize is that when a deadlock occurs during a negotiation, it's the negotiators responsibility to find a way to resolve it. A deadlock can have a significant impact on a negotiator's career in the following ways:

- You may get criticized by your own management.

- You may end up getting extra work in order to resolve this deadlock.

- You may lose your job.

- You may have a personal sense of failure.

- You may become frustrated.

- You may lose friends and damage relationships.

- You may make people angry with you.

- You may lose self-confidence.

- You may start to question your own business judgment.

So there is a lot of personal risk going on here. What's a negotiator to do? One key action that you can take occurs before the negotiations start. Every negotiation is really a team event – it's not just you sitting on your side of the table, it's really you, your team,Ã,Â and your management structure. If you take the time to discuss the possibility of deadlocks, what might cause them, where in the negotiations they might occur, and how best to deal with them then you'll avoid a lot of the consternation that a deadlock can cause your team.

One final point – don't give up just because you encounter a deadlock. In fact, the longer that the negotiations have gone on before the deadlock was encountered, the better your chances of being able to restart the discussions are. The more effort that has gone into the negotiations will mean that neither side wants to let a deadlock stop progress from being made...

Chapter 12

Deadlines Make Sales Negotiators
Give It All Away

Chapter 12: Deadlines Make Sales Negotiators Give It All Away

by drjim on June 23, 2009[edit]

Sales Negotiators Can Give It All Away In The End If They Are Not Careful

Every sales negotiation has some sort of time limit associated with it. You might have an hour, a day, or even longer to conduct the negotiations, but there is some point in time at which **you'll run out of time to talk**. This is when most sales negotiatlons fall apart.

The Problem With The End

Studies of negotiators has revealed a disturbing fact about all of us. During a normal negotiation we engage in a process in which we give a little bit and take a little bit. Pretty much what you would expect in any transaction. However, **then the news arrives**.

When we are informed or we become aware that the window to negotiate is **coming to a close** (perhaps someone important needs to leave for the airport), then for some weird reason one side or the other makes a mistake.

The Big Mistake

When we become aware of an approaching deadline, all too often we start to make big concessions to the other side of the table **that we wouldn't normally make**. What happens next is that they don't make big concessions to us, instead they make smaller concessions which causes us to make more big concessions.

It turns out that this type of behavior is practiced by both experienced and inexperienced negotiators. The only real difference is that the inexperienced negotiators made **bigger concessions** than the experienced ones did.

Why Do We Behave This Way?

In all honesty, this type of behavior really shouldn't come as a surprise to any of us. It all boils down to one simple fact of life: humans have a tenancy to make very bad decisions when we are **under pressure**. Clearly, the last few minutes of a negotiation is the worst time for us to be making concessions.

What To Do About It

If we can accept that we are poor decision makers when we are under pressure and if we don't want to give away the farm at the end of a sales negotiation, then what's a sales negotiator to do? In the end this is all about **self-discipline**.

You need to limit yourself to only making **small concessions** during the negotiation and you need to **space them out** during the negotiations instead of bunching them up at the end. As the end of the negotiations draws near, before you make **ANY** concession keep asking yourself:

1. Why should I make this concession, and
2. Can this deadline be negotiated?

If you can keep these questions in mind as the negotiations wind down, then you'll be all set to close better deals and close them quicker.

It's from the forge of failure that the steel of success is formed.

Hard Work Does Not Guarantee Success, But Success Does Not Happen Without Hard Work.

- Dr. Jim Anderson

Create An Effective Negotiating Team At Your Company!

Dr. Jim Anderson is available to provide training and coaching on the topics that are the most important to people who have to negotiate: how can my team effectively prepare for and execute a successful negotiation that will get us what we both want and need?

Dr. Anderson believes that in order to both learn and remember what he says, audiences need to laugh. Each one of his speeches is full of fun and humor so that what he says "sticks" with everyone.

Dr. Anderson's Negotiating Training Includes:

1. How to plan for a negotiation: what information do you need and where can you find it?

2. What's the best way to explore how a deal can be created during a negotiation?

3. How can you bring a negotiation to a close without giving in to the other side?

Dr. Jim Anderson works with over 100 customers per year. To invite Dr. Anderson to work with you, contact him at:

Phone: 813-418-6970 or
Email: jim@BlueElephantConsulting.com

60

57

Photo Credits:

Cover - By: James Butler
https://www.flickr.com/photos/slimjim/

Chapter 1 - By: frankieleon
https://www.flickr.com/photos/armydre2008/

Chapter 2 – By: Selbe Lynn
https://www.flickr.com/photos/stacylynn

Chapter 3 – By: Hector Alejandro
https://www.flickr.com/photos/hectoralejandro/

Chapter 4 – By: 401(K) 2012
https://www.flickr.com/photos/68751915@N05/

Chapter 5 – By: sota
https://www.flickr.com/photos/sota-k/

Chapter 6 – By: cosmo_71
https://www.flickr.com/photos/cosmok/

Chapter 7 – By: The Lamb Family
https://www.flickr.com/photos/lambfamilyphotos/

Chapter 8 – By: Jason Persse
https://www.flickr.com/photos/jasonpersse/

Chapter 9 – By: alacoolc
https://www.flickr.com/photos/42002245@N04/

Chapter 10 – By: hisham_hm
https://www.flickr.com/photos/hisham_hm/

Chapter 11 – By: Jeff Krause
https://www.flickr.com/photos/jeffkrause/

Chapter 12 – By: Timo D
https://www.flickr.com/photos/timosworld/

Other Books By The Author

Product Management

- Product Management Secrets: Techniques For Product Managers To Boost Product Sales And Increase Customer Satisfaction

- Product Development Lessons For Product Managers: How Product Managers Can Create Successful Products

- Customer Lessons For Product Managers: Techniques For Product Managers To Better Understand What Their Customers Really Want

- Product Failure Lessons For Product Managers: Examples Of Products That Have Failed For Product Managers To Learn From

- Communication Skills For Product Managers: The Communication Skills That Product Managers Need To Know How To Use In Order To Have A Successful Product

- How To Have A Successful Product Manager Career: The Things That You Need To Be Doing

TODAY In Order To Have A Successful Product Manager Career

- Product Manager Product Success: How to keep your product on track and make it become a success

Public Speaking

- Secrets To Organizing A Speech For Maximum Impact: How to put together a speech that will capture and hold your audience's attention

- How To Become A Better Speaker By Changing How You Speak: Change techniques that will transform a speech into a memorable event

- How To Give A Great Presentation: Presentation techniques that will transform a speech into a memorable event

- How To Rehearse In Order To Give The Perfect Speech: How to effectively rehearse your next speech to that your message be remembered forever!

- Secrets To Creating The Perfect Speech: How to create a speech that will make your message be remembered forever!

- Secrets To Organizing The Perfect Speech: How to organize the best speech of your life!

- Secrets To Planning The Perfect Speech: How to plan to give the best speech of your life

- How To Show What You Mean During A Presentation: How to use visual techniques to transform a speech into a memorable event

CIO Skills

- What CIOs Need To Know About Working With Partners: Techniques For CIOs To Use In Order To Be Able To Successfully Work With Partners

- Critical CIO Management Skills: Decision Making Skills That Every CIO Needs To Have In Order To Be Able To Make The Right Choices

- How CIOs Can Make Innovation Happen: Tips And Techniques For CIOs To Use In Order To Make Innovation Happen In Their IT Department

- CIO Communication Skills Secrets: Tips And Techniques For CIOs To Use In Order To Become

Better Communicators

- Managing Your CIO Career: Steps That CIOs Have To Take In Order To Have A Long And Successful Career

- CIO Business Skills: How CIOs can work effectively with the rest of the company!

IT Manager Skills

- Growing Your CIO Career: How CIOs Can Work With The Entire Company In Order To Be Successful

- How IT Managers Can Make Innovation Happen: Tips And Techniques For IT Managers To Use In Order To Make Innovation Happen In Their Teams

- Staffing Skills IT Managers Must Have: Tips And Techniques That IT Managers Can Use In Order To Correctly Staff Their Teams

- Secrets Of Effective Leadership For IT Managers: Tips And Techniques That IT Managers Can Use In Order To Develop Leadership Skills

- IT Manager Career Secrets: Tips And Techniques That IT Managers Can Use In Order To Have A Successful Career

- IT Manager Budgeting Skills: How IT Managers Can Request, Manage, Use, And Track Their Funding

- Secrets Of Managing Budgets: What IT Managers Need To Know In Order To Understand How Their Company Uses Money

Negotiating

- Learn How To Signal In Your Next Negotiation: How To Develop The Skill Of Effective Signaling In A Negotiation In Order To Get The Best Possible Outcome

- Learn The Skill Of Exploring In A Negotiation: How To Develop The Skill Of Exploring What Is Possible In A Negotiation In Order To Reach The Best Possible Deal

- Learn How To Argue In Your Next Negotiation: How To Develop The Skill Of Effective Arguing In A Negotiation In Order To Get The Best Possible Outcome

- How To Open Your Next Negotiation: How To Start A Negotiation In Order To Get The Best Possible Outcome

- Preparing For Your Next Negotiation: What You Need To Do BEFORE A Negotiation Starts In Order To Get The Best Possible Deal

- Learn How To Package Trades In Your Next Negotiation

Miscellaneous

- The Internet-Enabled Successful School District Superintendent: How To Use The Internet To Boost Parental Involvement In Your Schools

- Power Distribution Unit (PDU) Secrets: What Everyone Who Works In A Data Center Needs To Know!

- Making The Jump: How To Land Your Dream Job When You Get Out Of College!

- How To Use The Internet To Create Successful Students And Involved Parents

How To Develop The Skill Of Closing In Order To Get The Best Possible Outcome From A Negotiation

This book has been written with one goal in mind – to show you how to successfully close your next negotiation. It's not easy being a negotiator and so we're going to show you how to successfully close the negotiation in a way that will get you the deal that you want!

Let's Make Your Negotiation A Success!

<u>**What You'll Find Inside:**</u>

- **6 WAYS TO BREAK A NEGOTIATION DEADLOCK (PLUS ONE MORE)**

- **EVERY NEGOTIATION NEEDS A RAP(PORT) STAR!**

- **SUCCEED BY BRINGING THE GHOST WHISPERER TO THE NEGOTIATION**

- **A SALES NEGOTIATOR'S GUIDE TO DEALING WITH A DEADLOCK**

Dr. Jim Anderson brings his 25 years of real-world experience to this book. He's been a negotiator at some of the world's largest firms. He's going to show you what you need to do (and not do!) in order to get the best deal out of your next negotiation!